The Gardening Fires

The Gardening Fires

SONNETS & FRAGMENTS

Jérôme Luc Martin

WAYWISER

First published in 2015 by

THE WAYWISER PRESS

Christmas Cottage, Church Enstone, Chipping Norton, Oxon OX7 4NN, UK
P.O. Box 6205, Baltimore, MD 21206, USA
http://waywiser-press.com

Editor-in-Chief
Philip Hoy

Senior American Editor
Joseph Harrison

Associate Editors
Dora Malech | Eric McHenry | V. Penelope Pelizzon | Clive Watkins | Greg Williamson

A CIP catalogue record for this book is available from the British Library

ISBN 978-1-904130-66-6

Printed and bound by
T. J. International Ltd., Padstow, Cornwall, PL28 8RW

Acknowledgments

Grateful acknowledgment to the editors of the journals in which several of these poems first appeared: *Volt, The Colorado Review, Poetry London, Fence, Ambit, The Kenyon Review Online,* and *Stand.*

All day long
My heart was in my knee

– Herbert

Au réveil il était midi.

– Rimbaud

Contents

I

II

III

Contents

IV

I

Foxes First

Our stillness and the flaking stillness of that forest floor have
mouldered from the ear, but this you will remember: in the brief
reversing red of falling late November leaves, a volt of color
startled from the brake: a fuse laid into vanishing: a fox. Your
hands aquiver with the same escape, you caught the near branch
hanging there and through the shaking branch we saw it – not
a fox – a small coyote, running with its sandy coat lit up in
all the forging dense of sunset then that caught us up in motion
                                                    into motion –
here, here snow slips off the roof its pulverizing wing. The
weather keeps my letters from the post. The light drops through
the woods at evening, but I can't recross the still-dissolving threshold
of our second sight: I only see, descending on the hill, coyotes –
feral dogs – ourselves.
                    I would have brushed by lamplight foxes
from your hair; it has that red.

Foxes First

Our stillness – you

recross

The surgeon hand of sight – that separates

& sight – a scavenger – resumes

Dédicace

Dear, darling, dear heart, O my mort certaine, my almost
entirely voweled voie aurelienne, my roman road that
runs now next to what I know, that now lies stretching out
into darkness under – under the little loose rain of the morning
across the highway, across the valley, availed of your own
unbuttoned swiftness the maritime alps shake out their misty
rising pleats and, closer, in a pomegranate tree, their purple
catches at the husk of fruit the birds have shucked and
chambered through. The tree is really a thicket and lucidly
bare; the fruit hangs up in strips where day or night, day
or night, distance tears them on the branch.

And where I am
an airport hotel vaster in the ressac of jet-lag winds its rooms
around a central, heated indoor pool that waxes the glass of
hallway doors I buckle in to go to swim.

Dédicace

the saw's teeth scan the tapering branch –
the sawdust shakes and crumbles, where

from
where the sawhorse leans in wet grass dense among the pines, the
drifts of smoke of gardening fires – that double back and fill before
they rise –

direct our hesitation

Distance wears
its faceless obverse, layered hills

Too late I sent the letters on.

The noise of engines, patience, my
translations of Apollinaire (O mort certaine – O mes délices)
– the Alps on flight-maps, rings around me,
now

the sun has crept across my game of cards

inside the house
the winter sun is drying rabbit's bones upon my plate.

Dawn

It would have been your fingers – even unstill – even
unsure on my smooth blue dress-shirt collar just before
we walked into a room.
                          I woke into a night glazed with
machinery: the sleepers' lower deck, the ferry lit with
exit signs, the ghosts of islands, darkness out of which
two long, repeating lines of surf swept limestone fugitive
with gulls. Already, it was fading – that broad V of passage
stretched and spilled its final tier of quickness on the sea
somewhere outside Marseille – and in the distance, purple
loaded grey with its unprovable nearness. Hear me still,
where you sleep beneath green summits of the oaks:
the words I spoke the fusing morning, smoothing, steady,
recombines: *my dactyls are my loves, and nothing more;
my loves are dactyls, nothing more.*

Dawn

a roughening of oak leaves –

*brighter still, my hand inside the lamp throws rose-discolored
islands back to me*

*– the still-unlighted – white, still
unlit mountain of the ferry at the dock*

across the waves a drift of rose renews the pilot boat

an hour when even summer dust is wet with breath

*she drew the wet hair from her breast, as if to draw
and hold the feathered string*

Eclipse in August

Eclipse had a voice in the garden, falling, fading as my
secret summer notebook opened vaults into your knee
where you had opened it to read. The garden echoed, emptied
of cicadas – made its shadows in your ear. The doubled
sequence of an olive branch advanced to midday, misaligning –
moved your finger in the margin. I had written almost
nothing, but from ink the bees foamed up from purple beds
and cast a muscled shade: *my loves* – love carries up the
water from the well below the oubliette.

　　　　　　　　　　　　　　An hour before, your
heels in my hand, we'd fucked in the dark behind the day-latch
of an attic room, and rayed with vigilance and sweat
upon the half-tone reciffes of that feather bed you had – as if
to please me once again – had stretched one hand across into
the emberless blaze of the window-curtains.

Eclipse in August

your heels in my hand, my heartbeat at your knee,

its hour approaching stroked the valley noon

and smoky glass and cardboard

           and the voices carrying up from the garden, where
the little crowd that hushed and wandered on the walk – love
carries up

eclipse's second light: an aureole of shade aligning
pinpricked through a card

your light, sustaining ankles in my hand –

breathe – blow back from the bees that foamed up
out of purple beds – and cast again a muscled shade

Deluge

On bathroom skylight cobwebs, on the kitchen air, among
the cleaving wind chimes nailed up out of reach above the
porch steps, shower water stuck and beaded, scouting
down the walls . . . And outside, miles of rain were treading
the igneous globes of tulips past their prime, and lightning
ground the distance into surf that seemed to wash back from
your body gone back under in the distant flux and reflux
of the bathroom locks: oh, leave me, leave me, leave me,
we were calling.
       And in stillness then I heard you, hesitation
fresh against your skin, come close behind the door
and wait. And calling in the high air . . . gulls – a lost inland
concussive sound beyond the house. Then wind picked up
from your wet steps across the floor, and wind chimes
made a harmony I can't unsay.

Deluge

the hair that twisted down between your shoulder blades
was never dry

                                        The wind chimes made a
quarrel in the longitudes. All day

                                on dripped wet
hallway tiles – I weighed, in that imagined back and forth
of your wet steps, the obverse-reverse indecisions

                        cobwebbed steam, a skylight and the radio

                                in all the world, the
laving rearrangement of the refugees, the light-enduring
convex of your thigh,
                                and somewhere tanks across a border

                                neither one of us
– your wet hair coiling down your back

I can't unsay –

The Photograph

Those days, in that reflecting, mountain pine-scored light,
I thought I could look at you
secretly.
            Into a photograph taken that August your arm
now reaches holding a magazine open. We get
what we want. The darkness, after-dinner glasses, part
of a windowsill, part of a lemon tree, dusty flash-lit leaves like
tiles on an underground bath – across the mirrored pages of
Italian Vogue your arm shows tracing up beneath your tan
a slanting vein that nourishes the purple I remember: your
black nipple, naked in the sun: the purple of the
warrior fly that would not save itself.
                        Traversed by light,
traversable by light, we get what we want: our days without
quarrels, dewless, sweetworded nights – what we didn't
mean to have.

The Photograph

dear Agincourt, dear Dien Bien Phu

the glass verandah casts about the flies a trembling maze

                                 my pen retraces
pages cleaned by sun

                         the royal blue a drop of wine
to chase your slanting vein

Leave-taking

                          Grave, small, surefooted, where
the mountain path divides on rock, a herd of goats descending
split before me – soundless in the wind – though one was
haltered with a bell. And nightfall, quick on pink stones,
drove them down toward the covert or the pens. One stopping
in the juniper shook hard its little horns. Another stopped
and then, approaching, broke its damp, adept black muzzle,
took the salt out of my palm – love, brought me back
your quick and ragged tongue.

Leave-taking

of all my many months I am but one –

bright, early winter come again, and every apple
on the ground, and close friends murmur
parting in the road

great stations, sparrows under glass, and crated
southern palms . . .
                            arrival, like a hand that
taps a held breath –

firewood damp and loose in sleeves of bark

the curving halves that leap apart beneath the axe

                                the slow,
diffracting stroke of something now far out to sea
            or still as that volcanic plume
the pages rearranging years in binding rust

Not yet are you within

II

The Gardening Fires

How soon the gathered branches lose their sweat and resin
in the cloud, and fill with distance . . . Plumes of smoke
lift out of clearings, over shining greenhouse roofs:
above the alps, above the valleys, over that
white littered ground beneath the almond tree – the tree
that calls to mind the scent of those unmanageable
honeyed almonds burnt into a pan – all gather into
stillness, breathless, mingled clouds and smoke. And days
combine, a cloud of days.
                              Though I have been
attentive to the weather, to the strict wind, April's changing
seasons, any sign – among the stands of pines and stately
residential oaks – it's been so long, your living shade, when
it appears again among the burning leaves,
it even speaks unlike you.

The Gardening Fires

it's been so long that, as you are, and I

                              my long attention
fades the written ink; the days of weather clean
my page.

in cover of
the mountain pines

                         you wouldn't find me –

        where the quickly flaking coals revive,
a scent of resin wakes the taste of sweat:

that body, bridled smoke,

           a year's one day of snow along the coast
that powders off the branch – the way salt-water
salt would powder from your skin

The Ornaments

The feeding swan. The yellow jacket, hesitating in the
open window. Lemon trees – the rush of pasture – branches,
peach at points of newly broken wood. The page of
Birds of Shore & Sea we turned to – steel reflecting, station
platforms slipping past, and smoke blowing back on your
Hemingway coat. I turned to find the space to lift you up into
your bunk. You wore that necklace, gathered at your
collarbone. And tall in one another's arms, in drifting
railway sheets, our gestures still would intermix with, older,
tenderness. Our eagerness, the defter-handed years
would have.

        The chain devours its amber bead. The
hollow bridges – roughly long heptameters – the pear tree
growing through its net. The arching pin through all
I remember: your shifting intent.

The Ornaments

The dear, dear one
was naked, and she knew my mood. Their happier
days, the slaves of the moors.

the drift of beads, their untried measure

the poem starts 'the dear one', but for us, five years

that after dark that sound was smithied into light – the
towns, the gilded villages –

made perilous the longer use

the longer nights

The Rowers Hold Each Other

On water cleared of ice, that rosins oars above the surface
in the colder air, and cracks in oarlocks, our two boats
have slipped from narrow courses in the dark and closed, and
here, across a held-together space of rippled, dateless black,
among us two can stand unsteadily
and change places.
                              Equal, freed from rivalry, above
correcting oars in breath that gathers lifting off as from
a bath, they have to pass against each other, and the racing
shells are jarring side by side in likeness. Leaning close, one
rower starts to step apart: he holds the other's shoulders, then
his neck, his hand in warm hair curled above the nape, the
way – the way you slide the pear's two halves concealed
against each other in your hand – and how you gripped me
saying "close, too close, no more."

The Rowers Hold Each Other

now both have crossed and sinking, tie into their
angled foot-plates

Six is brushing drops of ice from Seven's splashtop. With
what strength we slip from what

                           refined by movements
passing through the eye of that exertion

ice – in turning sheets beneath the measured oars – had
narrowed arches of the bridge

                in turning sheets

                from us, retrieved by theft

the volatile, deliberate

repeated through translucent pages.

The Heron's Name

What we saw was this: the white of water struck
in middle distance near the shore – the bird's weight briefly
visible. Then big, folded wings unfolded, out-planted on
air and the cry went breaking through the early plates of
winter ice and echoes over water there re-fractured clouds
in rushes where the bird had stood. And someone
spoke the name.
                    I can't picture now the whole mud-beaded
head, the thatched and windy breast. I try to build the body up
from unfamiliar ossements – from instants in the reeds. I feather
flightless wings with water, each time making flashes of departure
for the feet. But just today, in mist that lifted off the cows'
backs, when I reached the stable's end and let the pail's brim
break and milk streaked down aluminum – that color
called the word back to my mind: it's *reiger, reiger.*

The Heron's Name

and floating intermix, the ice and reeds

You knocked a bead of
ink into my coffee cup – the first cold night
climbed both feet up my thigh

a snail-track mending ways across the garden

behind you, farther behind me, opened
whispered

Invitation

The night air pitching up and down the window tunes
a sliver openness above my ear. The windowsills are
dusted with lily – the park lawns littered with branches – my
holiday beard is rusting the basin – and, evading
the gaze of my round shaving mirror, a girl steals in on
tip-toes from the door. She breathes between my shoulder blades
and places – hardly to touch me – both hands on my back.
Do you remember, once, that both of us were searching for
the silver pin that drifted through your hair? And both
had our hands in your hair?
                    The girl has pushed the razor
from my cheek. I cannot see her face. We come here neither
one of us in confidence or care, and I, tonight myself
mistaking, named her you.
                    It has been raining all day long.
I'm living in Mawson Road.

Invitation

As if now to explain a hundred nights, your
slenderest presence

                              an inlay of pollen

your name – alarmless, plain

your name and summer, jointly constructed

                    worry the counseling mouth of the hive

The Captives

The lengthening delays of end-of-summer thunder passed
above the shuttered house, the windows loosely set
responding gently – fading into the sound of the pattering
threshold – and at last we stepped across to walk on golden
needles, soft and steeped into a noiseless carpet. Erica was
brushing drops of rain from Bruce's hair. And farther on, afloat
among the roses, wet, a single cloud – a garden table top,
its white untouched by shadows of the leaning pine – held up
for them two clear and brimming glasses.

                                    Love makes no
exchange of captives, even binding us when all that binds us is
their joy: not mine but ours, not yours or mine – the way
the summer lightning only seems to fan what it has struck,
what happened is hidden in blinding precision
from them, from us.

The Captives

that gathered in a lasting flash

                                        another,
lightning-feathered pine whose straightness softened –
resin shifting into air, near-weightlessness,

the intimate delays

                        that sealed

                refining years

the instantly refined,

beneath the leaking glass, verandah dust, refined in
summer floods and drought

                        diminish, hold

Your Littler Limbs

Your littler limbs than hers – the way that bright, American
midwestern spring in hindsight swells to fill its year – I felt
them stir the air above the bed, as if you were here, and Naike
got up and dressed.

                Outside, beneath the ravenous and
grey-backed gulls, beneath the harbor wall, a rower, drifting,
chews his callused hands. He takes again the turning boat's
one graceful and one stammering oar.

                          A little longer,
Naike lingers, twisting plastic shopping bags of fruit and
foreign bread. The market crowd of people weakens –
wavers – drifting like a month around me: once again, it feels
like you've come close – like I have been rewarded. Then,
again, before I stop or turn, as if to break the spell
the Arabs selling contraband cigarettes whisper behind me
"Marlboro, Marlboro," calling you back.

Your Littler Limbs

From hives of morning shadow, gulls

in poses close to sleep, you'd lain as if you stood upon the sheets –

turned over, gulls a shining pack of cards

the boat moves up into the wind beyond the wall

dear –

> *gentle –*
>
> *Naike's new dress keeps her in my sight*

– the waves break over, fill the closed stone.

The Urchin Shells

The hard bread hurt your mouth. Your lawless,
expectant flock of sparrows braided back the crumbs
along the ground. The inland mountain summer descending
scuffed the sand – and out beyond the rags of feather, foam
and glass were strings of whitecaps clasping, unclasping
October – October again. When you looked up, that pale
straw summer hat you sometimes borrowed drew its
lip of shadow back.
                What was that book that twisted away
on the rock, in the wind?
                All day I dove up urchin shells to
dry in the box in the kitchen, faintly scented under salt. By
streetlight at the window once or twice we took them out:
lit locks to further chambers – globes on which an
atlas roughness traced us back towards devotion. It was still
our irretrievable month.

The Urchin Shells

suspended in light from this quivering lens

that autumn – three more thousand miles of air
a wasp was chasing out and in –

the sand extending up among the pines – in places
brushed across the rails

in swift, unsettled, vandalizing progress, doubt

        beneath that fractured surface
urchin stairs of islands waver –

that September weather,

now Septembers touch the sands and go

Self-portraiture

Undressed at dawn . . .
At noon, the two days slip against each other, clouded
insides of a pear. Uncertain heights – and distances – adjust
a gull-defended shore, a vault of water sunk into the rock,
and set off somewhere, far above, the crackling of
loose stones.
My youth, delaying judgment, overtaken
by the things to come, no longer burnishes my idleness. All I
desired, accomplishing the slenderness of twenty-four and
twenty-five, attends another now. And now, uneasily revived,
ambition stirs – picks out designs that twist across a purple
towel blown out on the rock: a net . . . a stair . . . a net
more soot than gold – a stair that fills a darkened room,
descending from above – small-flowered, softly forged,
Hephaestos' net – the scholar's helical stair.

Self-portraiture

at twenty-seven, twenty-eight,

on open books my arm extending
flexes – warps like pages sealed by rain.

. . . and overtaken,
covered in a wagon with a purple cloak: my youth,
the last of those concentric embassies you held, the years
unsteady in their
symbols of reproach

your hair beneath a helm of salt

Conditions

My friends and those around me tire of this: these last
things dimpled by your elbows on the bed – the skylight
and the lightninged sheet.
                          It isn't dawn. The windows
lighten, white with climbing salt, and somewhere down below
the island gravels its beaches back from storm. The wind
is beating sticks of wild iris – channels in the limestone fill and
flutter with debris – and downy, worn with use, the sea
is unraveling under the high white side of a mediterranean
ferry approaching the dock. The ferry is turning – is tenderly
holding its face to the few harbor buildings – its wake is
expanding, passing by touch down the line of the small wooden
fishing-boats – please, love, in this light the chemical trail of
any strike-anywhere match could sweep into morning – in what
now is left let me slip from your mind.

Conditions

       salt, iris, thyme in flower, rosemary stiff with
bees

my palm was invisibly fuzzed by a barbary fig.

                    the crowds out on the dock
"It isn't dawn. I don't know where she is." – the clouds
up on the mountain

 raftered with debris

and surging in among the rocks between the quarantine
islands

            – when the boat stamped, you turned back: your
white-against-marine-white summer shirt that clouded

shivered, hovered, cotton
shaped on bone

snow, caught in summer altitudes,

stay – see the islands gravel back from storm
the wind comes shaving water to its ribs of foam

three thousand nesting pairs of gulls the mortise
all that we miss, all we pass out of

III

The Pines

Who came cold-fingered from the spring would not
have found me. The windfall clipped and sawn into a resinous
heap, and trodden deep, I'd gone in reeling with the vertigo
of pines: a tugged-at mind become one antlered by the
whip's-end lifting branches – green entanglements
and needle-patterned skin . . . and saplings in a strangling
clutch. I slept, and found on waking dripping pines
designed on mist.
                              Some years delay the fire that comes,
that feels its way unguided up the slope, through pin d'alep
and black pine fanning new growth – green surprised in
privacy – through branches long held heavy in sap or snow
and hushed in falling, quick to light.
                              The mist reveals
the nearness of the pines: their wading, human forms – the
bathers-in-the-hour . . .

The Pines

much later, Love in her apron of differing greys is
poaching pears

and neatly quarters glowing halves and slips them
into syrup,
              each a shining minute that extends in
sweetness, stitching at the loss of symmetry

in darkness, needles sweep into the sea of bark

                              the pin d'alep,
the corsican, the black pine boughs in wind

the way that time divides on pages

       apron loosely tied in winding strings

on one page, night and storm – and on another, afternoon: the
falls of ash so fine, they only show where
                              brushed –

and fires delay the flights along the coast

       again, again, the pears divide –

in rooms,

I write the way the wasps record their capture on the glass

The Hunter Fresco

In such a wood was I once in the bishop's chamber, love, as
this wet wood our rented Ford creeps up into, where alders
in the rain repeat the painted alders reaching up to limestone
weatherless inside that dome in Avignon. Where bark and
under-branches faded blue, and birds chalked airless channels
back to perch . . . and split off from the retinue of riders in the valley
and dismounted, one man, hand-high in a corner, brushed
an arrow to the string before the bared, in-songbird-branches-
antlered beast.
        Then you, beside me, brushed your sleeve across
the windshield and that misted-in, unviewing region opened on
our own windshielded selves. The night was falling; streaks
of city light were showing through a wood – through pathless
leaves and branches – what hand, once the hunter's hand is drawn
can still his feathered cheek?

The Hunter Fresco

We looked out through the traceries of wool on water;
glass brushed into regions

in the chamber, forests under cleared-of-weather
blue that fixtures grit of astres to the rock

what hand, when once

that alders in the rain – the painted alders

would have traced these words in ink across the facing
pages of your back one afternoon

the soap left honey in the stairs

and where, uncovered by the quick dawn in a clearing

Rhone between two lines of surf

September

September, come so close, was brushing back the fall
night sky with black on figs and grapes when, working late
beneath the garden wall, inside a ring of light and stones
I missed a stroke and knocked the chisel free. And half-blind,
one hand empty, staring out into the climbing ivy's
honed-with-lamplight closest depths, I caught the
recandescent scent the autumn's even stain would spring
from branches in the dark around me soon: that scent
retrieving days and gestures – that September when your
faint, unskillful perfume rose on smoke – when pinglints in
your clothing knew the bombings underway.
                                            Forgive me
if I speak as if despite – as if unchanged since then –
between the mountain air and many hands of
graveyard mint.

September

how they hold themselves

I found a shirt of yours among my things

*and stood in open sluices of the vines – was breathing held
by mountain air;*

– your many hands –

and breathing, shade on shade, as if

the point by point of safety pins undid

War Correspondence

Yes: your letter handed apricots into the crowd. Above
the village – in the mountains – into hands of children – in
my hands a thousand – miles away in this house, that
migratory firmness that you carried on your hips in green
cane baskets – opens me as opening above you, burning
campfire branches dimming, desert showed its high sides
caked with light. And later showed the bunchy, lunar silvers
on the burned limbs of the dead in Tel Aviv. "I saw them
dragged or carried across that wet, black square the market
crowd left empty, grimly fragrant in blown bales of
wheat." I have to see them too – through woven cane, your
beauty, apricots – and have to close the delta vault your mouth
made inside mine –
                         but all that I withhold here batters through
the market wall: *my loves*.

War Correspondence

something I would make a gift of

migratory firmness – frugal softness – something
sickening and fighting

delta vault of its first mouthful – this

pulled free, handed through the crowd

the gesture in the road beside sand-battered
camp-fire branches

that I trust this finds you

What I hold here – what I hold – in what

The Bull's Head Cup

This is the sculpted silver bull's head cup that,
tilted back to sip from, seems to drink or pause in drinking,
poised above a shaded pool its dripping muzzle still
disturbs – so lifelike that the drinker's breath expanding
on its hammer-chased, reflective surface dampens fuzz
along the dewlap, calling back a pulse of mist – so faithful
that the garland stamped around the rim, the edge of harness
leather, swiftly dissipating drops of wine remaining
crowd a scent that none can place, combining,
made uncertain in the made thing . . .

now, breathe in –

as if a few succeeding breaths could fix it, like
the orchard, having come up through the branches of
a hidden gap, you stepped in – into which you step –
the almonded, unalmonded air.

The Bull's Head Cup

its heel the joining lips; the lip a gilded harness
round the throat

the hammered hair between its nubs of horn (a tiny
hammer must have worked around its mind) in waves
a bit like mine, reflected in the laptop screen

and skating on its curvatures

an altitude, the swiftly dissipating

Love resumes its secrecy – a small boy hiding in the hedge

an axehead loosens in the grain of oak
and splits the knot at last with one long stroke

The Census

Reflections shape the narrow court, that shine from facing
windows now the sun has passed, and each unstoppered hour
seems less substantial, measured in the tracings of those
shadows cast by air in glass across my table . . . where
for days of this short stay my census trains the branch of thought
toward that master image, not unkind, of how
you were: bare-shouldered, shrugging in pleasure, nipping
the scored flesh of a mango from its skin, indulging in
the fantasy of love beneath your station – and, although
my written words catch up to your reply, your features
uncorrected, never to freckle.
                                        Hours before my morning flight
I puncture singing, crinkling cells of paracetamol. What lasts:
the dark new pinewood flushed and green with rain; the
island scrub of juniper that seemed immortal.

The Census

each summer since

the concrete stairs untouchable in full sun

tiled steps rising past a captive lemon tree

"control your sorrow"

cooled my hand against the door

*when you were still my guest the sound of shower water
running rushed my breath*

unready

in substance, springing up to die

Swim

Easy, easy, I heard my steps announced by the ice – a
tightening crowd. Here, swift and central currents whet
the thin ice open: rising, the river here steps
from its mantle – comes up through the kingfisher's
entrance – close to its visible edge, I heard applauding ice
beneath my feet.
              My nomad ice, the storm eluding report
between borders, you left your freckled white boots in the
roadside. Sleep was all night offering crumbling back
its edge: my hand inside the night-stand lamp
throws rose-discolored ices back to me.
                                      Come out. Come
out. An eagle is feeding the open water. Nearer the shore,
in an opening chopped with a wood-axe, shelves of broken ice
come back up flowsome, wet and rolling as for breath. My
beauty has even her bathing-cap off.

Swim

the snow locked up in bitterbrush a frozen mountain lake.

mine last, my

river – O my voyaging birchbark, light-enduring

come down from the tributary thaws

*   beneath my step that nerves – that now*
repopulates the ice

the sea draws its black velvet back from cuffs of foam.

Swimming the River

I did emerge, arduous with mud, my body plumed
with first leaves stirred from shallows, flushed,
seamed with gathered sunset in the run of water down
my skin, I touched the stones beneath the black
embankment slope; spring poured out from my mouth my
breast. Fasten these drops for my device: water wheeling the skin
away, exchanging air for air for months in the dry wind.
You stood over nettles, among white palings, once
while water trod my pulse, let me be
                                        faithful to you on
the other shore. I have barely got here but devotion,
this unsteady rose, leads me back down to surface
in that river where these words come up
not now between us but among those we love, not
each other.

Swimming the River

every time I lift my head here,
                              Natalie

            the testing stones

and now in longhand

starry clavicle – her clavicle – her scarred knee

IV

Before Wide Shadows

Night sky, golden vapor, green mimosa branches tied
back from the path – and dipping wands of olive, dipping
headlights through the gate . . . within, a table nearly set: your
hand was bleeding, held above a plate.
                                        At long last first
and last have closed, as if in rhyme. Before wide shadows
climb that hour with all the rest – before they fine remaining detail
from the cleanliness of years, and that vast substancelessness
passes, joining hollow to hollow in orbital dark – discard the
borrowed grace of injury, unpin your hair, accept
this equilibrium –
                    as if the two of us again
unwinding gauze unpacked the box of bandages . . . our
words and gestures fading with our vanishing regret: regret
that will not jog this welling progress – hands that drop
the iodine that stars the face of bread.

Before Wide Shadows

*Night sky, night sky, riders in soft-sanded woods, on
crossing trails*

      the pellet of a moon before the rings of Saturn

      stars – your features, foreign as willow honey

The Pelicans

And then, as if released from deeper zones of shadow in the air
and suddenly presented, cast along the phosphorescent, white
back line of breakers – where the pelicans would glide
untouched in troughs behind the surf – among the years, one
whole glad year had passed.
                              Friends – couples – visited,
made sweet the rims of glasses; weekends looped in pleasure, days
in study. Late at night, the city glowed onto the beach. And when
I saw you deep inside a restaurant, alive beyond my speech or
hearing, once, that year's refracting hem had long since swept from
smoothed or pitted sand. Now – love, our love, invention
of my long life – waves withdraw; the bay extends; the birds
brush open, feathered like the soft side of a paperback. The dead
on polished feet inscribe receding curvatures. The bones are
gulls' bones, porous, light past hollowness.

The Pelicans

the day without an apparition haunts my calendar.

           then motionless in flight, then pressing higher –
emissaries – shapes in their accustomed grey

           as if engraved, a line above a line, the pulse
on its uneven stairs

           the pelicans – the diplomats –
swift without intended haste, the message
insubstantial,

absence, steer me from above, beyond my range & state

 – "Stars are of mighty use"

           wet sand, and ashen softness

Notes

Dédicace: *"mort certaine"* Certain death. Words taken from Apollinaire. *"voie aurelienne"* A roman road following the coast of the Mediterranean from Rome to Pisa and eventually extending through southern France to Arles. *"ressac"* French word meaning "surf". "O mort certaine – O mes délices" Apollinaire again: *"O certain death – O my delights".*

Eclipse in August: *"reciffes"* From the French word for "reefs".

The Photograph: *"Agincourt"* Henry V's great victory during the Hundred Year's War, in which English archers decimated opposing French cavalry and foot. *"Dien Bien Phu"* Climactic siege during the War of Indochina.

Leave-taking: *"of all my many months I am but one"* Adaptation of a line from Rilke translated by Babette Deutsch: "of all my many mouths I am but one". *"not yet are you within"* From Melville's *Mardi.*

The Ornaments: *"The dear, dear one / was naked . . ."* After Baudelaire's "Les Bijoux".

The Rowers Hold Each Other: Seat racing is a training exercise used to determine the fastest combination of rowers. Two boats race – then, rowers from each crew trade places, crossing from one boat to the other. Then the boats race again. *"foot-plates"* The panels that bind a rower's feet to the boat. *"Six . . . Seven"* Rowers are commonly referred to by the name or number of their seat.

The Heron's Name: *"ossements"* From the French word for "bones". "reiger" The Dutch word for "heron".

Self-portraiture: *"a stair that fills a darkened room . . ."* From an etching by Rembrandt of St. Jerome. *"Hephaestos' net"* Hephaestos, the lamed blacksmith god of makers, was married to Aphrodite. He forged a delicate, nearly invisible net in which to catch his wife with her lover Ares. *"covered, in a wagon, with a purple cloak"* In some accounts, the Persian emperor Darius fled his final, decisive battle with Alexander in the back of an ox-cart. In the course of this flight, the emperor's bodyguard stabbed him to death and left him in the road. When Alexander came upon him soon after, he wept and covered his rival with his own purple cloak.

The Pines: *"pin d'alep"* French for the Aleppo Pine, *Pinus halepensis*, native to the Mediterranean region. *"the corsican"* Sub-species of the Black Pine or *Pinus nigra*.

The Bull's Head Cup: Greek, Asia Minor, 100 B.C.E. - C.E. 100

The Census: *"control your sorrow"* From Ovid's *Metamorphoses*.

Before Wide Shadows: *"Before Wide Shadows"* is also the title of a photograph of Saturn taken by the Cassini spacecraft in 2011.

The Pelicans: *"steer me from above, beyond my range & state // Stars are of mighty use"* From Henry Vaughan.

A Note About the Author

Born in the Netherlands, Jérôme Luc Martin grew up in Los Angeles and in the south of France. He holds a BA from Harvard University (2001). He completed an MFA at the University of Iowa in 2004, and a PhD in French and American literature (with a thesis on "restlessness") at the University of Cambridge in 2010. He now lives in London.

Other Books from Waywiser

Other Books from Waywiser

Deborah Warren, *The Size of Happiness*
Clive Watkins, *Already the Flames*
Clive Watkins, *Jigsaw*
Richard Wilbur, *Anterooms*
Richard Wilbur, *Mayflies*
Richard Wilbur, *Collected Poems 1943-2004*
Norman Williams, *One Unblinking Eye*
Greg Williamson, *A Most Marvelous Piece of Luck*
Greg Williamson: *The Hole Story of Kirby the Sneak and Arlo the True*

FICTION
Gregory Heath, *The Entire Animal*
Mary Elizabeth Pope, *Divining Venus*
K. M. Ross, *The Blinding Walk*
Gabriel Roth, *The Unknowns**
Matthew Yorke, *Chancing It*

ILLUSTRATED
Nicholas Garland, *I wish ...*
Eric McHenry and Nicholas Garland, *Mommy Daddy Evan Sage*
Greg Williamson: *The Hole Story of Kirby the Sneak and Arlo the True*

NON-FICTION
Neil Berry, *Articles of Faith: The Story of British Intellectual Journalism*
Mark Ford, *A Driftwood Altar: Essays and Reviews*
Richard Wollheim, *Germs: A Memoir of Childhood*

* Co-published with Picador